I0152837

COLOSSIANS

COLOSSIANS

THE GOSPEL, THE CHURCH,
AND THE NEW HUMANITY IN CHRIST

VIKA PECHERSKY

RESOURCE *Publications* · Eugene, Oregon

COLOSSIANS
The Gospel, the Church, and the New Humanity in Christ

Copyright © 2019 Viktoriya Pecherskikh. All rights reserved.
Except for brief quotations in critical publications or reviews, no
part of this book may be reproduced in any manner without prior
written permission from the publisher. Write: Permissions, Wipf
and Stock Publishers, 199 W. 8th Ave., Suite 3, Eugene, OR 97401.

Resource Publications
An Imprint of Wipf and Stock Publishers
199 W. 8th Ave., Suite 3
Eugene, OR 97401

www.wipfandstock.com

PAPERBACK ISBN: 978-1-5326-8237-7
HARDCOVER ISBN: 978-1-5326-8238-4
EBOOK ISBN: 978-1-5326-8239-1

Manufactured in the U.S.A.   APRIL 24, 2019

To Alan Vance

and

David Crason

God has willed that the restored creation should take form in, and in relation to, one man. He exists not merely as an example of it, not even as a prototype of it, but as the one in whom it is summed up. To participate in the new creation is . . . to participate in Christ

—OLIVER O'DONOVAN,
RESURRECTION AND MORAL ORDER

Contents

Preface

THIS STUDY EMERGED OUT of my strong conviction that deeper understanding of the written Word of God matters. If the intended meaning of the original author is the correct meaning, how serious am I about finding it. Is it possible to study Paul's letter and get to know him as a person? What were his hopes and fears for the Colossian church? What was his Spirit-inspired vision for their small Christian community? What part of Scripture did he meditate upon when he wrote this letter? Finally, how did Paul intend his audience to apply his teaching? At the end of the day, this study became an earnest attempt to think through the book of Colossians, asking and synthesizing difficult questions to push through the familiar knowledge of the book toward deeper insights and applications.

In my pursuit of this goal, I relied on the inductive Bible study method of observation, interpretation and application. I not only observed important words, grammar and sentence structure, but also paid attention to the use of literary devices, repetition of ideas and the development of the themes. Many of the study questions are intended to guide the reader through that process.

The interpretation step would not have been possible without the historical and theological expertise found in the Colossians commentaries of F.F. Bruce, N.T. Wright, and D.J. Moo. Posing interpretive questions and looking for patterns in Paul's writing along with earlier observations have also been instrumental in the interpretation stage. Thus, some study questions prompt readers to look at Paul's words through the lenses of larger themes and identify thematic connections within the text.

In the application stage, the initial aim was to understand how Paul wished his readers to live out his teaching and to look for ways of applying the whole book and its message, rather than separate passages. This approach would help ensure that application stays true to the original intent of the letter. Most importantly, my goal was to take the practical side of the letter equally seriously and pose questions, however hard they may seem, to help the readers connect their contemporary concerns with God's Word. Therefore, the application lessons are thematic and cover large topics within the letter to Colossians.

The study design may appear different from other Bible study guides, given the goal and the desire to take application seriously. Lessons one through nine are devoted specifically to the study of the text and discovery of the author's original intent. Lessons ten through thirteen are devoted exclusively to the application of the book of Colossians in the context of contemporary issues.

Finally, I have chosen the ESV translation for the purpose of this guide. It is a well-balanced translation that adheres closely to the original text and offers limited interpretation of the original words. All these elements should be tremendously beneficial to a study of this kind.

Overview of Colossians

Why study Colossians? Such a study might give the impression of an easy task given the book's relatively small and unassuming size. Maybe you chose Colossians because you have heard of its poetic descriptions of the excellencies of Jesus Christ and wanted to study them more fully. Some of you may simply seek a more practical goal, such as to make sense of your life, your faith, and the world around you. The book of Colossians can satisfy all these quests and many more. Though it is a small book written to a small house church in the first century AD, Paul's words have profound meaning and significance for the present day, the church, and the world.

Our current state of affairs as Christians is somewhat akin to where the Colossian believers found themselves two thousand years ago. Today, we are surrounded by different worldviews and rapidly changing ideas. Many Christians are a minority in their neighborhoods, cities, and countries. Most importantly, in the West, the threat churches face lies not in the open physical violence, but rather in shifting philosophies and worldviews that creep into our communities of faith, destroying biblical foundations. Similarly, this epistle addressed a community of believers caught amidst a world of competing ideologies, all vying for their hearts and minds. How could the young, vulnerable church of Colossae stand firm in its Christian theology and practices while being courted by the Roman Imperial cult, paganism, and Eastern mysticism? How were they to mature spiritually? How was their belief different from all those around them? Finally, was it any different from the Judaism of their day—the predecessor to their new faith? It is easy to imagine that there were as many Gentiles offering Colossian believers guidance on their spiritual journeys as there were Jews persuading them to be counted among the true people of God by becoming Jewish. It is in this context that Paul writes his letter. Its message is just as pertinent today as it was then: a message of encouragement to stand firm in the gospel of truth—the gospel of Jesus Christ.

PAUL THE AUTHOR

Throughout most of the history of the church, the authorship of Paul has gone uncontested.[1] Let us consider the direct clues offered in the text. Paul, the apostle of Jesus Christ, is named as the author in the opening of the letter (1:1). The letter ends with the statement: "I, Paul, write this greeting with my own hand" (4:18). Other secondary clues are woven throughout the letter. The author is imprisoned (3:3) along with Timothy and Luke, the beloved physician (4:14). Both men were known to accompany Paul during his ministry in Asia Minor. Other co-laborers and members of the Colossian community are named too, adding to the strength of the argument for Paul's authorship. Among them is Onesimus, who is also the subject of Paul's letter to

1. D. J. Moo, *Colossians and Philemon*, 29–30.

Philemon. The author mentions his suffering for the gospel (1:24), as well as his ministerial work of spreading the gospel among the Gentiles (1:27). These textual clues present a convincing case for Paul's authorship.

Aside from these technicalities, it is important to meet the person behind the words of this letter. Here is a man writing a powerful letter of both warning and encouragement to believers he has not met in person. We can see his enduring love and commitment to the gospel, the church, and above all, Jesus his Lord. He engages in a tireless effort to disciple young churches from afar until they are mature enough in their faith. We meet a man of deep conviction who does not lose hope in the cause of the gospel, even when he is imprisoned. Finally, we meet a man who serves his Messiah, Jesus, and understands the redemption narrative in which he and the burgeoning church have become active participants.

THE AUDIENCE

Paul's audience was a young house church in the city of Colossae (in modern-day Turkey). Most first-century churches consisted of small groups that met regularly in members' homes. The city of Colossae was located near the Lycus River Valley. It was once a center of thriving commerce, most notably as a hub for weaving and textile industries. However, at the time this epistle was written (circa 50–61 AD), it had lost its significance and much of its population to the two nearby cities of Laodicea and Hierapolis. All three of these cities were located near two major Roman highways that interconnected the province of Asia Minor. Close proximity to such busy roads meant that people in these cities were exposed to various beliefs and engaged in a free exchange of ideas. In part, this could explain why the Colossian church had to deal with other religious teachings.

Most of the population of Colossae, as well as the church, is believed to have been of Gentile origin. However, we know from other historical writings that the Lycus River Valley included Jewish communities that traced their history back to the Babylonian Jews.[2] Colossae has not survived to the present day and has not been excavated. Therefore, little is known about its everyday life and social makeup. Paul's letter, however, provides subtle details about the social and religious atmosphere that surrounded the church. He points to the pervasive moral decay rampant among Colossians (3:57) and an active religious scene, in which certain groups challenged and argued with the believers of Colossae (2:4) in order to persuade them to embrace their own philosophies (2:8). Unsurprisingly, we can also sense pressure from the Jewish community to rely on the Jewish ceremonial law (3:16) as a means of demonstrating their faith. This pressure seems to have originated both from inside and outside the church. Paul's request that his letter should be read in Laodicea hints that similar problems were present there as well (4:16).

In short, we can conclude that Paul's audience consisted of a small community of mostly Gentile believers who, while stable in their faith (2:5), were subjected to various social and religious pressures that could potentially derail their community and dilute their faith.

THE LETTER

Several important points must not go unnoticed concerning the nature of the Pauline epistles, and Colossians in

2. F.F. Bruce, *Colossians, Philemon, Ephesians* 8–12.

particular. While they may sound obvious, overlooking them could lead to misunderstandings, not to mention improper applications of the text.

First of all, this letter, like most of Paul's writings, is an effort to disciple these believers—to bring them to maturity and teach them to obey everything that Jesus had taught, even though Paul could not disciple them in person. Second, this letter, just like the other New Testament epistles, has a very practical purpose and was written for a specific group of people. While Colossians certainly includes substantial teachings about the supremacy of Jesus and His work of redemption and reconciliation, the purpose was not merely to convey general knowledge. Paul wrote it to help the Colossians lead everyday lives that reflected the image of Christ. Finally, Paul wrote this letter specifically for the church of Colossae as a whole. It was not meant to simply foster individual spiritual growth. He wanted the entire group to know the truth so that they could, in a certain way, act together as a church—a community of faith. In fact, the role of the church was crucial to Paul's admonition of Colossians. All his teaching was aimed at the community, its identity, and its practices.

What all this means is that the message of this epistle is closely tied to the situation of the Colossian church—namely, the appearance of false teachings, which Paul characterizes as philosophy (2:8), mysticism, asceticism, the worship of angels, dietary restrictions, and adherence to Jewish festivals and the Sabbath (2:18). It is unclear from the text and there is no consensus among scholars as to whether Paul is referring to a single set of teachings or various belief systems. Yet one thing is clear: these teachings claimed to offer certain ways of attaining personal spiritual maturity. They were seeping into the Colossian community, resulting in a real threat to their understanding of truth and their ability to live it out practically. While the threat may have come from individuals, the damage could affect the entire church. Paul was well aware of the similar dangers affecting other churches (Gal 5:7–10). In response, he wrote an exposition of the gospel of Jesus Christ, showing his supremacy in God's redemptive work, offering an ultimate narrative for the whole creation, not just an alternative path to personal spiritual heights.

Several major themes play important roles in Paul's exposition. These include the person of Jesus Christ, the gospel itself, knowledge and wisdom, creation, redemption, reconciliation, the church, and godly living with thanksgiving. Other more subtle but immensely important references to the account of creation, the human mandate, the kingdom of God, the Jewish temple, peace, truth, and human maturity are also present. I hope that in the course of this study you will learn to recognize them in the text and understand how Paul weaves these threads into the message for the Colossians.

The Study

These thirteen lessons will immerse you in a rich Biblical narrative. You are encouraged to dig deeper to learn from God's Word. Lessons one through nine will guide you through the study of the letter itself. Lessons ten through thirteen are devoted specifically to the application of the truths that should become evident over the course of this study. The study guide is designed this way in order to help you spend sufficient time thinking through the application for both yourself and your church.

The two goals for this study are to examine the epistle within the greater biblical narrative, and stay faithful to the practical purpose of this letter. The first goal stems from humble attempt to understand Paul's words within the larger biblical storyline. The themes upon which he draws in this letter go as far back as the first chapters of the book of Genesis. In the course of this study, you will attempt to understand where these themes originated and how Paul applied them to Jesus and the Colossian believers. The study questions will offer an opportunity to think through some of the larger topics of the Bible and investigate how Paul connected them to build an argument for the sufficiency and supremacy of Jesus. The second goal stems from the deliberate effort to seek personal applications in this present day. Specially designed assignments will encourage you to examine your life based on the message of Colossians, as well as various philosophical movements, in order to bridge the temporal distance between the original recipients of this epistle and contemporary situations.

THE OUTLINE OF COLOSSIANS

1. 1:1–2—Greeting
2. 1:3–12—The gospel of truth
3. 1:13–23—The gospel of Jesus
4. 1:23–2:5—Paul and the ministry of the gospel
5. 2:6–23—Threat to the gospel and the church
6. 3:1–17—A new creation living by the gospel
7. 3:18–4:6—A well-ordered creation
8. 4:7–18—Final instructions

Homework

1. Read the entire letter to the Colossians, paying attention to what Paul says about Jesus, the gospel, and the church. As you read, write down all you observe about:

Jesus

The gospel

The church

2. In one paragraph, write a summary of the book of Colossians.

3. Read Gen 1–3 while paying attention to the themes of creation, temptation, and the fall of Adam and Eve. Write down your summary of these events. A lot of Paul's writing in Colossians can be traced back to the opening chapters of the Bible. It is possible that the story of creation and the fall offered the divine inspiration for much of Paul's writing in the book of Colossians.

LESSON 2

1:1–2—Greeting
1:3–14—The Gospel of Truth

THE FIRST CHAPTER OF Colossians includes one of the best-known verses in the New Testament. In this lesson you will trace Paul's thoughts leading up to his magnificent proclamation of the glory of Jesus Christ in verses 15–20. First, let us start at the very beginning.

GREETING (1:1–2)

The letter begins with a formal salutation—*i.e.* an opening paragraph where the author names himself and the audience to whom the letter is addressed. This opening is standard for the Roman epistolary tradition, which usually includes the author, the audience, and a greeting. It is also short and simple in contrast to the verses that follow. We get the impression that Paul is in a hurry to get to the things he wants to say in the following verses. Write down each as it appears in the text.

Author—

Audience—

Greeting—

The Gospel of Truth (1:3–14)

Col1:3–14 contains Paul's thanksgiving and prayer for the believers of Colossae. His prayers are usually rich and dense. They often serve as a plot diagram for the rest of his letters, touching upon the main themes and the purpose of his writing. This prayer is no exception. The next few lessons will match the intensity of Paul's writing as you attempt to unpack the meaning of his words.

1. Read verses 1:3–14. List what Paul is thankful for on behalf of the Colossians in verses 4–5.[LL a-c]

    a. . . . in Christ Jesus

    a. . . . that you have for all the saints

    b. . . . laid up for you in heaven

What can these characteristics tell us about the Colossian church?

From the opening thanksgiving prayer, we learn that the young church of Colossae received high praise from Paul, the kind any church of today would be eager to receive. Notice that they had *faith*, *love*, and *hope* because of the word of truth—the gospel (v. 5). Paul pauses his prayer before continuing to speak on the topic most dear to his heart. He tells the Colossians in verses 1:3–8 that the gospel they understood and received as truth has not only reached them but is in fact spreading around the world, *bearing fruit and increasing* (v. 6). It has been noted by biblical scholars[1] that these words represent a close Greek translation of the

1. G. K. Beale, *The Temple and the Church's Mission*, 264.

Hebrew phrase found in Gen 1:28, when God blessed the first humans and gave them the mandate to be *fruitful, multiply,* fill the earth, and subdue it. The fact that Paul uses the same phrase again when he resumes his prayer in verses 9–14 suggests that Paul's thoughts indeed could be traced all the way back to the first chapters in the book of Genesis, which depict the creation of mankind in God's image and outline the purpose he laid forth for human beings. God commanded Adam and Eve to fill the earth and reign over all creation as His representatives. Paul then tells the Colossian believers that, through the gospel of Jesus Christ, this mandate is being fulfilled. The gospel is spreading around the world, bearing fruit, and multiplying through people who themselves bear the fruit of godly living and increase in the knowledge of God. This is not the only reference to the creation account found in this epistle. In the course of his letter, Paul returns to God's act of creation several times in order to help his readers understand who Jesus is, what God's plan for this world is, and what their new identity in Christ is.

2. Read below Paul's prayer for the Colossians (1:9–14) in light of the previous verses that refer to Gen 1–3, the human mandate, and the spread of the gospel around the world:

> And so, from the day we heard, we have not ceased to pray for you,
>
> asking that you may be filled with the knowledge of his will in all spiritual wisdom and understanding,
>
> so as to walk in a manner worthy of the Lord, fully pleasing to him:
>
> bearing fruit in every good work and increasing in the knowledge of God;

being strengthened with all power, according to his glorious might, for all endurance and patience with joy;

giving thanks to the Father, who has qualified you to share in the inheritance of the saints in light.

He has delivered us from the domain of darkness and transferred us to the kingdom of his beloved Son, in whom we have redemption, the forgiveness of sins.

Paul prayed that the Colossians would have the *knowledge* of God's will in all spiritual *wisdom* and *understanding*. These three words are used together throughout the Bible. God created the universe with knowledge, wisdom and understanding (Prov 3:19–20). They belong to God (Dan 2:20–22), who gives them to whom he pleases. They are the marks of his chosen people (Deut 4:4–8) that set them apart from the rest of the world. They qualify people to rule over Israel (Deut 1:13, 1 Kgs 3:8–10) and to be truly human (Ps 49).

3. In light of the situation in the Colossian church and the verses above, what was Paul praying for when he invoked "knowledge, wisdom, and understanding" in his prayer?

4. Read Col 1:9–11. How do knowledge, wisdom and understanding relate to godly living? What are the ends and what are the means? Look carefully at the way Paul structures his sentence in verses 9 and 10.

5. Based on Paul's prayer, what makes a believer's life worthy of God and pleasing to him?

6. In his prayer, Paul describes people who possess the knowledge of God's will, live godly lives with which he is pleased, and are transferred into the kingdom of the beloved Son. Look for ways Paul's vision for these people reflects the story of creation and the fall of Adam and Eve (Gen 1–3). Start by listing the similarities you notice between the first humans and believers in Christ.

7. What do these believers now have that humans lost in the fall? Compare Gen 3:23–24 and Col 1:13–14, 20.

Truth, knowledge, and wisdom are words that have deep biblical meaning and play a key role in the story of creation and fall of man. In the opening chapters of Genesis we learn of God, the creator of the universe. He also created humans in his image to rule over his creation. God alone possesses the totality of knowledge and wisdom. However, God made his will freely known to the first humans. God revealed his purpose for their lives and what they were to do or not to do. He dwelt with them in the garden so they could seek knowledge and wisdom from him when they needed to live and fulfill their mandate. Yet we know that Eve was seduced by a promise of a certain knowledge with Adam following suit, rendering them unable to dwell in God's presence and fulfill their calling. They were separated from an intimate relationship with God and exiled from the Garden of Eden, and they bore the consequences of their sin.

Paul's thanksgiving and prayer for spiritual knowledge and godly living ends with the foundation on which it is built—the redemption God the Father has achieved for us through his beloved Son. The concept of redemption traces its origins back to the dark times of slavery. It was commonly used to describe the process by which a slave paid off what he or she owed in order to purchase his or her freedom. If another person paid the ransom on the slave's behalf, that person was called a redeemer (Ruth 2:20). In biblical terms, the word *redemption* represents God's act of paying the ransom in order to free his people from physical and ultimately spiritual slavery.

8. Read Appendix I about the biblical concept of the inheritance of the saints. Read Col 1:12–14 and break down, point by point, the message of redemption.

Write each clause on a separate line. Following the example below, make note of persons of the Godhead, verb tenses, and pronouns.

giving thanks to the <u>Father</u>,

who has qualifi<u>ed</u> <u>you</u> to share in the inheritance of the saints in light.

What have you learned based on these observations?

In the biblical narrative, following the fall of the first humans, the redemption became foundational in God's relationship with people. The first time "redeem" appears in Scripture is when God addresses Israel just before the exodus from Egypt (Exod 6:6). In the Old Testament, the redemption of Israel from Egyptian slavery and the subsequent settling in the Promised Land was considered to be one of the most important acts of God since creation and the fall of mankind. The similarities between the first humans in Eden and Israel in the Promised Land are hard to miss. Most of the major Jewish religious practices and festivals, such as Passover, The Day of Atonement, and Sukkot, retell Israel's story from the point of their redemption from the Egyptian slavery. That is when God created a nation for himself—a people for his own possession—by freeing them from slavery. God gave them land and wisdom in the form of the Law, so that he would once again dwell (Exod 6:5–7) among the people who were just and holy (Deut 4:5–8). However, in the course of the biblical narrative, we learn that slavery of a different kind has always been a far worse enemy to human beings, including the Israelites—*i.e.* slavery to sin. Therefore, Israel was in need of the ultimate redemption and forgiveness of sins along with the rest of the world.

9. Read Gen 1–3, Exod 6:2–8, Isa 59:9–20 and Col 1:3–14. In your own words, map out the storyline of redemption culminating in Jesus.

Gen 1, 2—

COLOSSIANS

Gen 3—

Exod 6:2–8—

Isa 59:9–20—

Col 1:3–14—

1:15–23—The Gospel of Jesus (Part One)

WE LEARNED IN THE previous lesson that Paul, in his prayer, connects important events in the history of mankind, namely the creation and ultimate redemption through Jesus Christ. He connects them via the gospel of truth, in order to provide a powerful vision for the Colossian believers—a vision of the renewed humanity spreading around the world, possessing wisdom and knowledge of God and able to lead a life pleasing to him. Paul lays out a global view for his readers how they have been redeemed from their slavery to sin, forgiven through Jesus' sacrificial death on the cross, accepted by the Father into the Son's kingdom, and increased around the world through the gospel.

Then Paul turns his eyes to the Son who embodies the truth. Our verses for the next two lessons contain one of the clearest passages regarding the sufficiency and supremacy of Jesus found in the New Testament. It is firmly believed that verses 15–20 represent an early Christian hymn that Paul incorporated into his letter. These verses are full of poetic references and rich imagery. Each line is packed with biblical meaning that carries cosmic implications. Overall, the language of the hymn is deeply creational, and it is best viewed through the prism of the creation and fall narrative. At the same time, the immediate context of Paul's prayer for knowledge, wisdom, and understanding should also be taken into consideration when you interpret these verses.

1. Break down verses 15–20 and write out what they say about Jesus. Follow the example below.

    He is the image of the invisible God,

    the firstborn of all creation.

    For by him all things were created, in heaven and on earth, visible and invisible, whether thrones

2. What observations did you make after breaking down the text of the hymn?

In light of what we have just learned about Paul's prayer, it is not surprising that the hymn hailed Jesus as both the Creator of the world and the Redeemer. Paul once again conveys his global vision of the gospel and reveals how, in the person of Jesus, the gospel seamlessly connects creation and redemption of the people of God into one narrative for the whole world.

In this lesson, you will dive deeper, focusing specifically on verses 15–17. The hymn starts with the following phrase: "He is the image of the invisible God." These words can be interpreted in several ways. The following paragraph will offer three possible readings. However, in the Old Testament, the phrase "the image of God" (the true God, not false idols) applied exclusively to human beings—specifically, the first humans, who were created to be representatives of God on this earth (Gen 1:26, Gen 5:1, Gen 9:6). Old Testament law permitted no other image of God. In the New Testament, it is applied to both Adam and Jesus (2 Cor 4:4, 1 Cor 11:7). In his writings, Paul compares Adam (as a representative of all humans) to Jesus on several occasions. Paul establishes parallels and contrasts between Adam and Jesus to explain the purpose of Jesus' incarnation, presenting him as a perfect human who, unlike Adam, stayed faithful and obedient to the Father and reversed the consequence of Adam's sin (Rom 5:15–19, 1 Cor 15:20–26).

Therefore, one possible interpretation of the phrase "image of the invisible God" is that it refers to Jesus, given that he was a perfect human being, as a true Adam. Alternatively, in Rom 5:14, Paul states that Adam was the "type of the one who is to come." Therefore, another possible interpretation is that Adam was made in the image of Jesus.[1] Last but not least, this phrase may mean that Jesus is God's true representation, the one who reveals God for people

1. D. J. Moo, *Colossians and Philemon* 117–118.

to know—something Jesus himself taught in his earthly ministry (Luke 10:22, John 1:18, 14:9).

3. Based on these possible interpretations and immediate context of chapter one, what do you think the phrase *"He is the image of the invisible God"* means? Explain.

4. *The firstborn of all creation.* In Scripture, the word *firstborn* is used both literally, meaning the order of someone's birth, as well as figuratively; for example, it can signify Israel's elevated status above other nations and the right to an inheritance (Exod 4:22). Since this word is found in a poetic context in Colossians, it is reasonable to conclude that it is used here as a figure of speech. Read Prov 8:22–23 and Col 1:15–6. Write down the parallels you observed.

5. *For by him all things were created, in heaven and on earth, visible and invisible, whether thrones or dominions or rulers or authorities—all things were created through him and for him. And he is before all things, and in him all things hold together.* This sentence is a continuation of the previous line of the hymn. It presents Jesus as a creator and the supreme ruler over all creation. Read Col 1 and Prov 8. List all the parallels you see between these passages.

6. What does the allusion to God's wisdom communicate about Jesus?

7. Think about how the first lines of the hymn reveal Jesus in light of the situation in the Colossian church as well as Paul's prayer for knowledge, wisdom, and understanding. Write down your answer.

1:15–23—The Gospel of Jesus (Part Two)

In the first half of the hymn, we see Jesus portrayed as a true image of God on this earth, as the Wisdom of God for the fallen humanity, the creator and ruler of everything that exists, both visible and invisible. Let us examine the second half of the hymn in verses 1:18–20 and look at the complete portrait of Jesus Christ. Read verses 1:15–20.

1. *He is the head of the body—the church.* Notice that the notion of headship over the church follows the theme of supremacy over creation. What is the connection between these two themes?

2. *He is the beginning, the firstborn of the dead, that in everything He might be preeminent.* This line follows closely that of verse 15b and presents Jesus as not only the creator of everything that already exists but also the beginning of a new creation that commenced at his resurrection. Write in your own words how Jesus' resurrection, new beginning, and preeminence over all creation connect together to paint a magnificent portrait of Jesus.

3. *In Him all the fullness of God pleased to dwell.* The language of this line is full of references to the tabernacle and Jewish Temple, where God's glory dwelt.[1] Read Ps 68:16, Exod 29:43–46, Ps 43:3, and Ps 132:13–14. How does the language of the Temple and God's glory dwelling among his people apply to Jesus?

1. G. K. Beale, *The Temple and the Church's Mission*, 267.

4. *Through Him to reconcile to Himself all things . . . making peace by the blood of His cross.* This line flows out of the previous one, so we can paraphrase it as the fullness of God is pleased to dwell in Jesus, and through him, to reconcile to himself all things by the blood of the cross. We see Jesus as both the temple where God's glory dwells and the sacrifice upon the altar. How does this verse point to the climax of the redemption narrative by connecting Jesus to Adam as well as Israel at the same time?

This hymn is indeed a poetic song that proclaims Jesus to be the Divine Lord of all. Yet it does so not by appealing to the Greco-Roman philosophy of logic or Near Eastern mystical ideas of their time, but by using Old Testament language. It is rooted in the way God is revealed throughout the Scriptures. Jesus is hailed as the God Israel already knows—the creator and redeemer of his people, the Lord over all creation, the wise One who dwells among his people. He is the Lord who is intimately involved with his creation, yet supremely preeminent. This hymn flows out of Paul's prayer as an anchor of faith for the Colossians. Paul encourages them to rest in the fullness of Jesus, because in him, they have the wisdom and knowledge of God who created the world, redeemed Israel, and now, once and for all, has brought the story of mankind to its intended climax and a new beginning.

5. Read Col 1:21–22. How do these verses support both Paul's prayer and the hymn?

When it comes to interpretation of Paul's words to the Colossians, it is important not only to look closely at each word and sentence, but also to view his whole letter as a piece of literature that has its own pattern, flow, and the development of the theme. Paying attention to the repetition of words, themes, and ideas can help you take hold of Paul's train of thought and trace how he develops it. For example, look at the beginning of Paul's prayer in 1:5–8 and immediately after the hymn in verses 1:21–23. Read these passages side by side below. Both of them share the same themes and similar sequence. Both express, in parallel terms, how the gospel gives hope and spreads around the world. Therefore, the theme of the gospel serves as a framework to interpret what Paul says in between these two passages. In other words, the prayer and the hymn contain the meaning of the gospel.

Colossians 1:5–7	Colossians 1:21–23
because of the hope laid up for you in heaven. Of this you have heard before in the word of the truth, the gospel, which has come to you, as indeed in the whole world it is bearing fruit and increasing—as it also does among you, since the day you heard it and understood the grace of God in truth, just as you learned it from Epaphras our beloved fellow servant. He is a faithful minister of Christ on your behalf.	*And you, who once were alienated and hostile in mind, doing evil deeds, he has now reconciled in his body of flesh by his death, in order to present you holy and blameless and above reproach before him, if indeed you continue in the faith, stable and steadfast, not shifting from the hope of the gospel that you heard, which has been proclaimed in all creation under heaven, and of which I, Paul, became a minister.*

6. Based on verses 1:3–24, in your own words, write down what is the gospel of Jesus Christ.

1:24–2:5—Paul and the Ministry of the Gospel

THE GOSPEL IN PAUL'S prayer and worshipful proclamation of Jesus lays the foundation for everything he discusses in the rest of his letter. In the previous lessons, we learned about the good news of a perfect man and the divine Lord in the person of Jesus, who is the creator of everything that already exists as well as the beginning of a new creation: the church, the redeemed people of God who are reconciled to God by Jesus' blood on the cross. The redeemed have every reason to be thankful; they have been transferred into the kingdom of the beloved Son. They have ultimate access to the wisdom of God and knowledge of how to live a life pleasing to him. As Paul wrote in Colossians, the gospel was spreading across the world through Jesus' body—that is, the church, carrying a message of reconciliation and redemption. Of this gospel, Paul became the minister. He then turns attention to his own ministry on behalf of the church.

1. Read Col 1:24–2:5. Observe and write down the words and themes that Paul has already mentioned in the previous verses.

It is possible that the situation of the Colossian church motivated Paul's choice of words in this passage. A teaching was circulating in and around their community of faith that was mystical and ascetic in nature. However, Paul's discussion of his sufferings in the flesh and the mystery of the church appear in his other writings and is not unique to this letter. Before you study this passage, it is important to remember that Paul has just talked about the sufficiency and supremacy of Jesus in the redemption of his people. Therefore, when Paul speaks about making up for what is lacking in Christ's afflictions, you can be assured that he does not refer to Jesus' death for our sins. It is best to try to understand these verses in their immediate context, which is Paul's discussion of his mission on behalf of the church to spread the gospel around the world.

2. Read 2 Cor 1:5–6 and 2 Cor 4:10–12. How do these verses add to your understanding of Paul's words about his sufferings in Col 1:24–25?

3. Read verses 1:26–29. These verses are eschatological in tone, which is usually employed in the end-times passages. Speaking of things that have been hidden for ages and are now finally being revealed is a defining trait of eschatological literature (Matt 10:26–27, Luke 17:29–31, Rom 8:18–19). Verses 26–29 fit right in the middle of Paul's overall discussion of the gospel that is being preached in all of creation (1:6, 23) and of Jesus being the final fulfillment of the redemptive history (2:9–15). What is the mystery to which Paul refers?

4. How does the language of mystery—that here refers to the work of the Messiah spilling over the borders of ethnic Israel to fill the rest of the world—show God's plan for his creation? Try to answer in light of Paul's earlier allusions to the creation and human mandate.

5. What is Paul's definition of the goal of his ministry in 1:28–29? Write Paul's description from these verses word for word.

6. What is the goal of reconciliation achieved by Jesus Christ in 1:21–22? Compare it to the purpose of Paul's ministry and write down what you find.

7. If the goal of both Jesus' and Paul's ministries is a collective holly and mature humanity, what are the signs of human maturity based on these passages? Answer with specific words and phrases as they appear in 1:21–22, 28–29, and 2:1–4.

8. In his prayer, Paul prayed for the Colossians to be filled with the knowledge of God's will in all wisdom and understanding. How do verses 2:1–4 help us understand his prayer and what he meant by God's will?

9. Observe the tone of Paul's words in 2:1–5. How would you describe it? What troubled Paul? What positive signs encouraged him?

10. Paul wrote this whole letter of warning and admonition even though the church appeared to be stable where believers had faith, love, and hope. Why do you think it was not enough? Try to answer in light of the opening prayer and the way Jesus is portrayed in the hymn.

11. Based on all you have studied so far in the book of Colossians, what is the church? Be comprehensive, and refer to the text to support your definition.

2:6–23—Threat to the Gospel and Church

In the previous lesson, we learned that Paul aligned his ministry with the work of Jesus and the purpose of reconciliation through Him. Paul strove to continue what Jesus started until the gospel reached the whole world. Just like Jesus, he sought the renewal of humankind by helping people to become complete and mature in Christ. The time had come for God to reveal his ultimate plan for the coming of his Son and to reach all the people of the world. Paul was at the helm of this laborious and dangerous mission, one full of joy and divine power. We also got a glimpse of Paul's tender care for the Colossian church and his concern for their spiritual well-being. In this lesson, we will examine the reasons for his concern in greater detail.

1. Read 2:6–23. To sketch the general view of the threatening teaching, observe and list the elements of false teaching on one side and Paul's arguments against them on the other.

Elements of false teaching	Paul's arguments

2. In verses 2:6–7, Paul gives his first command in this letter. What is it? Look for connections between Paul's first direct command and his opening prayer in 1:9–12.

3. Paul never quotes the words of Jesus in this letter; however, it is important to pay attention to the way Jesus' ministry and teaching is reflected in Paul's writing. How does Paul's command draw on Jesus' words in John 15:1–11?

4. Read 2:8–15. In verse 8, Paul described the teaching that was threatening the young church as:

   1.

   2.

   3.

   4.

5. What is Paul's response to this "empty philosophy" in verses 9–15? How does Paul build his argument while knowing there might be Jews in the audience? Make sure to note his use of verb tense in his response. Try to retell his argument in your own words.

In his argument against the teachings threatening the church, Paul refers to two major Jewish symbols: *circumcision* and *baptism*. Why does he include these two concepts to build his case for the sufficiency of Christ? Is it possible that the teaching threatening the Colossian church was Jewish in nature? Circumcision and baptism are deeply symbolic, each in its own way. Both were part of the practices of the Old Testament covenant people of God—the

Jews. Circumcision symbolizes the covenantal relationship between the Israelites and their God (Gen 17:9–11). It was instituted by God as a physical sign of their chosen status that symbolized the cutting of the flesh that got in the way of complete obedience to God. Israel was given a promise that the Lord would one day remove the flesh from the heart of his people, and they would love and obey him with all their heart and soul. They would not be destroyed, but rather, live (Deut 30:6).

Baptism, while never prescribed by Jewish Law, became an important ritual of cleansing and consecration before anyone could enter into God's presence (*i.e.* in the Temple) for prayer or sacrifice. In contrast to circumcision, which was performed only once, baptism was practiced regularly by devout Jews as penance for sins or for ritual cleanliness. Baptism therefore symbolized repentance from sins and the purity needed to be worthy in the presence of the Lord. Circumcision and baptism were performed together in one particular instance: when a Gentile converted to Judaism. Both rituals, along with a sacrifice, served as a rite of initiation into the household of God. This rite was in essence a reenactment of Exodus—Israel's transformation into God's holy nation, which had occurred through circumcision, the sprinkling of sacrificial blood of the Passover lamb, and finally, freedom from slavery through the waters of the Red Sea (encapsulated by baptism). After this initiation rite, the person was not only considered to be a Jew but also a newborn child; he or she would start a new and holy life, totally disconnected from the past.[1]

---

1. J.K. Howard, *New Testament Baptism,* 12–21.

6. How does this historical context underlying circumcision and baptism help us understand Paul's argument?

7. Paul's exposition of Jesus' supremacy in 2:9–15 echoes 1:15–20 and 1:21–23. Read these passages. What does Paul focus on this time?

8. In verses 16–23, Paul issues two warnings to the Colossian believers. Write them down word for word as they appear in the text. What do they mean, and how would they come across—specifically for the Colossian believers?

   1.

   2.

LESSON 7

3:1–17—New Creation Living by the Gospel

THE COLOSSIAN CHURCH FACED pressure from religious groups to conform to certain ideas of what mature spiritual people were supposed to be and do. These believers were told that they should follow a set of ancient traditions and teachings, participate in festivals, and keep the Sabbath. They were also supposed to have dreams and visions, worship angels, and achieve new spiritual heights by subjecting their physical bodies to their will through extreme deprivation. Paul gives a twofold rebuttal to such notions. First, some of these practices were mere shadows of the fulfillment, which is Jesus himself. Second, while they may have appeared wise, all of them failed to deal with the main problem that plagues human beings: the inability to control the sinful flesh. Therefore, Paul dismisses all the aforementioned attempts as foolish. Jesus is the ultimate divine Wisdom for men because in him, we have all we need; he resolved that problem of sinful flesh by his death on the cross. Jesus has paid the ransom. Nothing else is needed in order to reconcile people to God. Those who receive Jesus are renewed and brought into a new state of humanity, lacking nothing. However, this is not just some abstract construct without any bearing on people's physical existence on this earth. Far from it. In this lesson, you will study how Paul expounds what living as a new creation in Jesus means when it comes to everyday life.

1. Read 3:1–17. Look for the themes of the new human-ity, the image of God, reconciliation, thanksgiving, and wisdom. Note how Paul applies them to the Colossians' new humanity in Jesus Christ. How would you put this into your own words?

2. Compare Paul's teaching in 3:1–17 to the practices of-fered to the Colossians by other religious groups in the previous chapter. What differences do you see? Note that in both cases, there are things to do and not to do. What in your opinion is at the core that differenti-ates the gospel of Jesus from what the other teaching offered?

3. Using 3:1–17, write in the left column what believers are "to put to death/away" and in the right what they are "to put on." Compare and detail your observations.

"Put to death/away"	"Put on"

4. Based on Paul's teaching in 3:1–17, why is moral purity in the church important?

5. Read 3:1–2 and 2:6–7. How does Paul expand on his first command?

6. Paul describes the Colossians' new identity as:

3:1—

3:10, 11—

3:12—

Summarize their new identity in your own words.

7. It is important to bear in mind that Paul's teaching about living as a new creation is addressed to the whole church—not just individuals. Paul's vision of a new creation is decisively communal. Read 3:1–17 and identify new practices that Paul encourages them to cultivate.

8. Notice that throughout the book of Colossians, Paul applies the concept of love specifically to the members of the community of faith. Read Col 1:8, 2:2, and 3:14. What is the role and importance of love for fellow believers in the church, according to Paul's teachings in Colossians?

9. How does Paul's teaching about love reflect the teaching of Jesus to his disciples (John 13:34–35, 15:12–17)?

10. Thanksgiving is an important concept that Paul repeats over and over in this letter. Read Col 1:3, 1:12, 2:6, 3:15,16,17, and 4:2. What role does thanksgiving play in the lives of redeemed and renewed people of God?

11. According to Paul's teaching in Col 1:21–22, 28–29, the goal of redemption and the work of the gospel is to create mature humans around the world. Paul's vision for human maturity is collective in nature. In this letter so far, Paul taught Colossians that the death and resurrection of Christ has launched a new beginning for the human race. Jesus created a new humanity, a new body—the church that united people of all races and ethnicities, slaves and free into one. Based on Paul's teaching in 3:1–17, describe other traits of maturity humankind.

Unity,

3:18—4:6—A Well-Ordered Creation

JESUS HAS REDEEMED HIS people; their lives are now hidden with him in God. When he is revealed in glory, so will they be revealed in him. This is the hope of the future that believers receive through the gospel. The life of the believer now is a life of substance and goodness, which is found in Jesus himself. It is the life of transformation into his image. The things believers do as God's people are not merely symbols or rituals, but constitute a daily living out of the new identity with eternal qualities that do not fade away; this is true even in the simplest of tasks. Those being renewed are united in Jesus by love that transcends ethnic, social, or cultural differences. They now live a communal life full of thanksgiving, wisdom, and praise. This is the new creation of which the Colossians became a part. In this lesson you will see that just like when God brought order into chaos in the Genesis creation, so is the newly created humanity called to live well-ordered lives. One of the striking features of this lesson's passage dealing with the Household Codes of their time is how structured and ordered Paul's instructions are. Here Paul takes the Greco-Roman guidelines that were generally used to outline social and political structure of society and looks at them through the prism of the gospel. Paul retains the overall structures of the family and society intact, showing the ordered nature of God's creation, where everyone is ultimately subjected to God. Paul did not call the renewed people of God to cause chaos or dismantle social institutions, but instead to redeem them from within by following in the footprints of Jesus Christ. Paul calls Colossian believers to live in this world but to be not of this world, just like Jesus (John 17:10–19).

1. Read 3:18–4:6 and write down the categories of people Paul addresses. What struck you about the groups of people he included or the corresponding instructions?

2. Paul's instructions to family members are clear and direct. Write down what Paul addresses to each member of the family.

3. How might Paul's instructions to the fathers be different from the family codes of that time?

4. Is there any difference between the word "submit" in Paul's injunction to wives and the word "obey" in his command to children? If so, explain.

5. How do these instructions to the family uphold the order established by God in creation (Gen 1–2)?

6. Paul gives more detailed and nuanced instructions to the slaves in verses 22–25. Write down his instructions. How does Paul encourage the slaves? Compare verses 17 and 23.

7. What does Paul demand of masters? What are the full implications for those who are in charge? How does this reflect the orderly nature of creation?

8. How does Paul tell Colossians to behave toward "outsiders"—people outside the church? Paul addresses both conduct and speech. How is it different from his instructions regarding the treatment of fellow believers inside the church, as stated in earlier verses?

9. What are the final, general commands for Colossian believers in verses 4:2–4?

10. Based on everything that Paul has taught the Colossians so far, why does he end with these words of admonition, as opposed to something more active—*e.g.* calling them to fervent evangelical pursuits, abstaining from worldly pleasures, or catalyzing social and political change?

4:7–18—Final instructions

CHRISTIAN LIVING DESCRIBED BY Paul in his letter to the Colossians is remarkably simple and unglamorous. Generally speaking, there are no magical acts, no exciting visions, no fascinating stories about angels and spirits, no mysterious rituals, no extreme bodily exercises, nor even traditions that go back millennia as a support for a claim to spiritual superiority. However, the gospel of Jesus Christ offers something deeper and more profound. It offers truth, reconciliation, wisdom and knowledge of God, renewal, and a community of faith bound by love. In this community, there is purity, goodness, forgiveness, patience, and order. At the center of it all is the person of Jesus Christ, in whom all these things are found. Even if the letter to the Colossians were the only extant book of the New Testament, we would have sufficient knowledge of both the gospel and how to live a meaningful, Christ-centered life. In the course of this letter, Jesus is portrayed as the reason for everything ever created, including the church. He is the ultimate Wisdom, the Creator, the One through whom the Father redeemed and renewed his people. We have learned that the church is a bodily representation of Jesus on this earth, called upon to bear his image with purity, unity, love, and thanksgiving. The ending of Colossians is just as remarkable as the text preceding it. Paul finishes with an enlarged section devoted to their local matters, as well as final greetings.

1. Read 4:7–18. Write down each person or group of people Paul mentions and how he describes them.

2. What can we learn from the way Paul described these groups? Note also the use of "one of you" (ESV) and "Jews" (ESV).

3. How does Paul's description of Epaphras reflect the purpose of the whole book?

4. After completing the study of the letter, write down your summary of the book of Colossians. Compare it with what you wrote at the beginning of your study.

The Application of Paul's Teaching in Colossians

THE GOAL OF THE next four lessons is to focus on how Paul's words to the Colossians apply to our lives today. Application of biblical truth is both simple and complicated. In many cases, what needs to be done is rather obvious and not difficult to discern. For example, the Household Codes of 3:18–4:1 are very direct and need no extensive efforts to find God's will for our marriages or parenting. They simply need to be followed in our everyday lives. However, we often fail to move from knowing to doing. This dilemma exists for many reasons. One has to do with philosophy, or a certain way of thinking. Western Christianity became a religion of personal internalization. Supposedly, as long as one knows and understands the gospel, nothing else is required. Mental apprehension of the truth became paramount at the expense of a strong community of faith, godly obedience, and prayer.

What would Apostle Paul tell our churches today? How would he apply the truth of renewed creation in Jesus to our current state of affairs? The following lessons will help you tackle some aspects of these questions as you turn your attention to your lives.

Assignment 1

Read Appendix II about the Nicene Creed. Imagine that you are part of the Colossian community, which was under constant pressure from other teachings. Your group is given the task to write what your home church believes based on the truths revealed in this letter. Take some time to think through what you have just learned, and write your statement of faith in at least six sentences.

1.

2.

3.

4.

5.

6.

Assignment 2

Write your own declaration of intentions and actions based on the teaching of the book of Colossians. Choose one of the main themes listed below and elaborate in a few sentences. Consider it prayerfully while writing.

1. Jesus Christ is the source of our spiritual wisdom and understanding.

2. We are a new creation, made in the image of Jesus to reflect it to the world.

3. We are part of the church—Jesus' bodily representation on this earth.

4. We are part of a community of faith where there are no more ethnic, cultural, or social barriers, but Jesus is all in all.

1.

2.

3.

4.

5.

LESSON 11

Thanksgiving and Prayer

HOW DID PAUL WANT his audience to live out his teachings in Colossians? In short, he called them to live a Christ-centered communal life full of purity, unity, and love, to carry out an orderly life in their society, and lastly, to devote themselves to prayer—to stay alert in it and have an attitude of thanksgiving. The biggest application question we need to pose and meditate upon is this: "Why, after giving such a cosmic and global view of Jesus and the church, does Paul offer such localized and down-to-earth application?" In the following lessons, we will begin thinking about what kind of Spirit-inspired vision Paul had for the life of the renewed people of God. We will examine some of these topics in the following order: first, we will look at thanksgiving and prayer, then living in relation to the world, and finally at living in a community of believers.

Thanksgiving

If we were to decipher how Paul intended the Colossians to apply the contents of his letter, we would inevitably come across the idea of thanksgiving and gratitude. From the first chapter to the last, Paul repeatedly exhorts Colossian believers to be thankful. How can gratitude help us stay faithful to Jesus amidst an onslaught of different teachings and philosophies? In other words, can gratitude help us stay faithful to Jesus? Perhaps Paul intended to show that being thankful takes us back to Jesus as the ultimate source of everything we have and will ever need. Gratitude is the attitude of the heart that rests in sufficiency. It means, "I don't need anything else; I have all that I need." This is exactly what is at the heart of Paul's epistle to the Colossians—Jesus is the fullness of all that we need.

Assignment 1

1. Write down what you are thankful for based on the teaching of Paul in the book of Colossians. Try to be as specific as possible.

2. Rate yourself on a "thanksgiving meter" from one to ten. One means, "I seldom thank God in prayer or conversation with other believers," while ten means, "I regularly include thanksgiving in prayer and conversation with other believers." Ask yourself why you rated yourself as you did and write down your answer below. Make sure to include thanksgiving in your daily spiritual practices.

1_____10

3. Write down what you are usually thankful for. Seek the Lord to help you expand this list and look for ways you can speak with thanksgiving in your community of faith.

Prayer

If you were addressing a group of believers who were in danger of submitting to teachings other than those of the gospel, would devotion to prayer be one of the things that you would most strongly urge them toward? In his final words, Paul calls the believers of Colossae to devote themselves to prayer. Intriguingly, he is talking about the entire church here—not just its individuals. Why pray together when you are in danger of temptation? Remember when Jesus asked His disciples to stay alert and pray for Him in the Garden of Gethsemane? Those who read the Gospels' accounts know that they did not. Praying can be hard work, but Paul says that this is how we must stay alert in this world. Paul also gives Colossian believers the example of Epaphras, who labors for them in prayer.

Assignment 2

Think of what you should choose to devote yourself to in prayer. Try to find a prayer partner or group that meets regularly to pray, and labor together with them.

Philosophies, the World, and the Church

WE SWIM IN A sea of competing ideas and philosophies. We live in the midst of cultural wars and social turmoil. All this has shifted and swayed public opinion to an unimaginable extent in the last decade alone. Churches, of course, have not been immune to these changes. Young people are leaving their communities of faith. This mass departure occurred in part because of the ideas they were exposed to in schools, universities, the news, and social media, as well as the often inadequate reactions of the church to its own shortcomings and the world around it. The matter at stake for churches in the West today is not what it means to be genuine people of God, but rather what it means to be genuinely human. What is often lacking in our discourse is a clear and coherent teaching that addresses what the church is and its responsibility to the world around it. Does the book of Colossians contain anything that might help us in our current situation? Can it help us come away with a clearer understanding of what it means to be a new creation in Christ and what we are to do in this world? After all, what is the gospel if not a message to preach around the world for all creation under heaven?

Paul's teachings for the Colossians, especially those in chapter three, are more relevant to our current times than ever. Paul teaches that to be renewed in the image of our Creator (3:10) is to be genuinely human. The church united by love consisting of genuine human beings who are being renewed into the image of Jesus Christ is the real life picture of what the whole world will look like. Yet it must start within the church first, not outside it.

We have to ask Paul some hard questions in order to come up with ideas to apply when we try to relate to the world around us. Why does he not teach the Colossians to actively involve themselves in the world and fight against the social injustices, such as slavery? Perhaps he does? If so, in what ways does he teach them to do so? Of course, the believers of Colossae could not vote for the laws that they thought were more moral and just, nor could they elect the candidates that were most representative of Christian values. What if they could have? Would Paul's admonition have been any different? Finally, is Paul drawing upon what he learned from Jesus himself and his earthly ministry when he speaks to the Colossians about what it means to be a new creation in a conflicted world, still largely bound by slavery to sin?

Assignment 1

Take some time to contemplate and answer each of the questions above as best as you can. Think in light of Paul's teachings about the church, how it should be defined by love, unity, moral purity, and orderly living. Finish the following statement as a way of summarizing what your responsibility to the world is as a Christian:

I am part of the new creation, and my responsibility to the world is:

Assignment 2

1. Try to identify the major philosophical movements that affect us today. For example, Platonism, Gnosticism, Modernism, Postmodernism, Atheism, and Nationalism. Write down each of them and define their principal tenets in your own words. How do they affect your faith and your church?

2. Based on Paul's teaching in the book of Colossians, what do you need to know and do in order to withstand negative influences of such philosophies?

Lesson 13

Living in the Community of Believers

THE LETTER TO THE Colossians may seem small and unassuming. However, it is much larger in the scope of its vision than its size suggests. Paul paints a canvas that offers a bird's-eye view of God's purpose for the whole world, from its very beginning to the present time. He employs themes that delve deeply into the history of God's purpose for man and his plan for man's redemption. Jesus is revealed as the reason for everything that God has done throughout history—all that for a small house gathering in Colossae. Although Paul's audience was a small house church in a city of little consequence in the heartland of the Roman Empire, this community of believers clearly mattered to Paul, regardless of its size and location. That small group of Christians was just as important as any other, because it was part of the body of Christ. These believers were participants in the new creation that was set in motion by the death and resurrection of Jesus—the new creation that proliferated around the world through the gospel of truth. Paul framed all the practical aspects of the Colossians' new lives in the context of a community of believers who live out this reality together. This final lesson will be devoted to the church—the body of Christ.

1. If asked why the church is important, based on what Paul wrote in this letter, how would you answer?

2. How important is your church community in your own life, both spiritually and socially? Explain your answer.

3. Would you say you love your church and the people who attend it? Explain your answer.

4. How do you already show or plan to show your love for the saints in the context of your local church?

5. According to Paul's teaching in 3:1–17, the community of believers should be characterized by moral purity and integrity. Look back on the list of what Paul calls the Colossian believers to "put away" and "put on" in lesson 7. Try to identify those that apply the most to your own life.

6. How would you personally apply Paul's teaching about the church—a unified community that breaks social, cultural, and ethnic barriers (Col 3:10–11)?

Inheritance of the Saints

THE IDEA OF THE inheritance of the saints is tied directly to God's covenant with his people, *i.e.* those who belong to God and enjoy a special relationship with him that sets them apart from the rest of the world. It is also deeply connected to the redemption of God's people from slavery and their transformation into a nation obedient to its creator and redeemer. The Lord redeemed Israel from slavery to create a new people for himself; they became his inheritance (Deut 4:20). He gave Israel a special status in his creation as the kingdom of priests who live in his presence and proclaim his glory to the rest of the world.

> There Israel encamped before the mountain, while Moses went up to God. The Lord called to him out of the mountain, saying, Thus you shall say to the house of Jacob, and tell the people of Israel: 'You yourselves have seen what I did to the Egyptians, and how I bore you on eagles' wings and brought you to myself. Now therefore, if you will indeed obey my voice and keep my covenant, you shall be my treasured possession among all peoples, for all the earth is mine;

> and you shall be to me a kingdom of priests and
> a holy nation.'—Exodus 19:2-6

The Israelites became God's own people, his children. As such, the Lord gave them an inheritance of their own (Exod 6:7–8): the Promised Land that they came to possess. In this land they would dwell in God's presence and perform the calling for which the Lord had redeemed them. After the division of Israel's kingdom into Israel and Judah and the subsequent fall of Judah to Babylonian captivity, the inheritance of God's people came to mean not just possession of the Promised Land, but participation in God's kingdom that rules over all the inhabitants of the earth (Dan 7, Matt 5:5, 25:33–35; Rev 5:9–10).

> And they sang a new song, saying ,"Worthy are
> you to take the scroll and to open its seals, for
> you were slain, and by your blood you ransomed
> people for God from every tribe and language
> and people and nation, and you have made them
> a kingdom and priests to our God, and they shall
> reign on the earth."—Revelation 5:9–10

APPENDIX II

Nicene Creed

PAUL WROTE HIS LETTER to the Colossians with a long-term goal in mind. Judging by the high praise it received from Paul (Col 1:3–5, 2:5), the church of Colossae was stable and thriving. What else would they need, we might ask. However, Apostle Paul, inspired by the Spirit, foresaw that the influences of other teachings and philosophies that had begun to close in on the church would have a corroding effect should they be left unchecked. Therefore, he wrote a letter that is rich in theology and grand in its scope, built around the divine person of Jesus who defines not only our origins and future destiny, but also our existence now in our physical bodies on this earth. All this is to say that the gospel of truth encapsulated in correct theology and practical living was of great importance to Paul because it insured that the long-term renewing work that Jesus had started and he, Paul, had become the minister of, was being carried on by the church.

Fast forward almost 300 years, and the church found itself dealing with the question of correct theology on a much larger scale. In 325 AD the representatives from major churches across the Roman Empire gathered together in the city of Nicaea (in modern-day Turkey) to discuss a theological controversy that was tearing up the church. That meeting became known as the Council of Nicaea. The cause of the divisions was Arianism—the teaching of Arius, one of the bishops of Alexandria. Arianism denied the full divinity of Jesus Christ (and of the Holy Spirit) and presented him as a created being, begotten from God the Father.[1] As a result, the Council condemned Arian teaching as heresy and created a document called the *Nicene Creed*. It is an essential statement of faith that outlines the correct doctrine and teaching of the church. The final version of the document was completed in 381 AD and is also known as the *Nicene-Constantinopolitan Creed*. Besides the holy canonical Scriptures, this is the only theological document accepted and affirmed by all the branches of historical Christianity.

> I believe in one God,
> the Father almighty,
> maker of heaven and earth,
> of all things visible and invisible.
> I believe in one Lord Jesus Christ,
> the Only Begotten Son of God,
> born of the Father before all ages.
> God from God, Light from Light,
> true God from true God,
> begotten, not made, consubstantial with the Father;
> through him all things were made.
> For us men and for our salvation
> he came down from heaven,
> and by the Holy Spirit was incarnate of the Virgin Mary,

1. Beeley and Weedman, *The Bible and Early Trinitarian Theology*, 187–188.

and became man.

For our sake he was crucified under Pontius Pilate,

he suffered death and was buried,

and rose again on the third day

in accordance with the Scriptures.

He ascended into heaven

and is seated at the right hand of the Father.

He will come again in glory

to judge the living and the dead

and his kingdom will have no end.

I believe in the Holy Spirit, the Lord, the giver of life,

who proceeds from the Father and the Son,

who with the Father and the Son is adored and glorified,

who has spoken through the prophets.

I believe in one, holy, catholic and apostolic Church.

I confess one Baptism for the forgiveness of sins

and I look forward to the resurrection of the dead

and the life of the world to come. Amen.[2]

Bibliography

Beale, G.K. *The Temple and the Church's Mission: A Biblical Theology of the Dwelling Place of God.* New Studies in Biblical Theology. Downers Grove: InterVarsity Press, 2004.

Beeley, Christopher, A., Weedman, Mark, E. *The Bible and the Early Trinitarian Theology.* Studies in Early Christianity. Washington DC: The Catholic University of America Press, 2017.

Bruce, F.F. *The Epistles to the Colossians, to Philemon, and to the Ephesians.* The New International Commentary on the New Testament. Grand Rapids: Eerdmans, 1984.

Catechism of the Catholic Church. Second Edition. Vatican: Libreria Editrice Vaticana, 2000.

Howard, J.K. *New Testament Baptism.* London: Pickering & Inglis, 1970.

Moo, Douglas, J. *The Letter to the Colossians and to Philemon.* The Pillar New Testament Commentary. Grand Rapids: Eerdmans, 2008.

O'Donovan, Oliver. *Resurrection and Moral Order: An Outline for Evangelical Ethics.* Grand Rapids: Eerdmans, 1986.

www.ingramcontent.com/pod-product-compliance
Lightning Source LLC
Chambersburg PA
CBHW071104090426
42737CB00013B/2473